ADA TWIST, SCIENTIST
THE WHY FILES

ALL ABOUT PLANTS!

By Andrea Beaty and Dr. Theanne Griffith

Amulet Books • New York

*To the many, many talented people
who have helped Ada on her adventure
from page to screen. Thank you. —A.B.*

For my mother —T.G.

PUBLISHER'S NOTE: This is a work of fiction. Names, characters, places, and incidents are either
the product of the author's imagination or used fictitiously, and any resemblance to actual
persons, living or dead, business establishments, events, or locales is entirely coincidental.

Library of Congress Control Number 2021946115

ISBN 978-1-4197-6151-5

ADA TWIST ™ Netflix. Used with permission.
Story and text © Andrea Beaty
ADA TWIST series imagery © Netflix, Inc. and used with permission from Netflix.
Ada Twist, Scientist and the Questioneers created by Andrea Beaty and David Roberts

Book design by Charice Silverman
Illustrations by Steph Stilwell

Printed and bound in U.S.A.

10 9 8 7 6 5 4 3 2 1

Amulet Books are available at special discounts when purchased in quantity for premiums and
promotions as well as fundraising or educational use. Special editions can also be created to
specification. For details, contact specialsales@abramsbooks.com or the address below.

Amulet Books® is a registered trademark of Harry N. Abrams, Inc.

Images courtesy Shutterstock.com: **Cover:** *sunflower*, Radoslaw Maciejewski; *watering can*, Nerthuz;
cherry blossoms, Emilio100; *plant*, violetkaipa; *dirt*, domnitsky. **Pages i, 3 (*leaf*), 4, 20, 36:** Jr images.
Page 8: *dirt*, Nataly Studio; *fruits*, Natalia Lisovskaya. **Page 9:** Zen S Prarom. **Page 10:** Kobkit Chamchod.
Page 15: Casther. **Page 19:** wavebreakmedia. **Pages 21, 57, 72, 75:** Green Leaf. **Page 34:** *snowy
tree*, Andrey tiyk. **Page 39:** Nature Clickz. **Page 40:** *sunflower*, Radoslaw Maciejewski. **Page 46:** Brian
Maudsley. **Page 47:** *leaf*, The Gallery; *dirt*, Nataly Studio. **Page 48:** Sardo Michael. **Page 58:** Herrieynaha.
Page 60: Koy Jang. **Page 62:** Boris Medvedev. **Page 64:** Nataly Studio. *Images courtesy Public Domain:*
Pages 2, 40 (*apples*), 45 (*apple tree blossoms, daylily*): George Chernilevsky. **Page 3:** *cactus*, Laitche.
Page 11: *potatoes*, MarkBuckawicki; *carrots*, congerdesign. **Page 16:** Ho Nguyen Han. **Page 17:** *green
trees*, The Frog001; *yellow trees*, Mshuang2. **Page 18:** Wanda Sisk. **Page 29:** Tbk1101. **Page 34:** *green
tree*, Thomson200. **Page 44:** *rose*, Huhu; *hibiscus*, ShinyButton. **Page 49:** J Zapell. **Page 52:** Alabama
Extension. **Page 65:** Ksd5. *Images courtesy Creative Commons:* **Page 26:** *tree*, Bruce Marlin; *waffles*,
TheCulinaryGeek. **Page 37:** Paul Shannon. **Page 35:** "Evergreen Forest" by Image Catalog. **Page 53:** Becky
Matsubara. **Page 61:** David Ohmer.

ABRAMS The Art of Books
195 Broadway, New York, NY 10007
abramsbooks.com

MIX
Paper from
responsible sources
FSC® C002589
www.fsc.org

I see a tiny flower in the crack of the sidewalk! Why is it there?

It's a mystery! A riddle! A puzzle! A quest!

Time to find out what plants are about!

1

Plants are found all over the world. They can grow on mountains and underwater. Plants also come in many shapes and sizes. But they all have the same main parts.

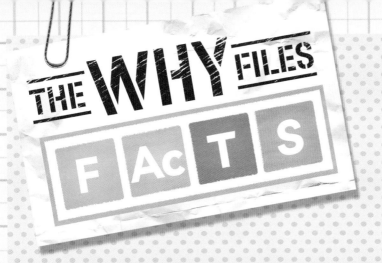
PARTS OF A PLANT

- **FLOWERS**
  (Not all plants have flowers.
  But most do!)

- **STEM**

- **LEAVES**

- **ROOTS**

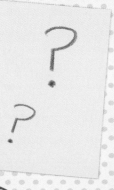

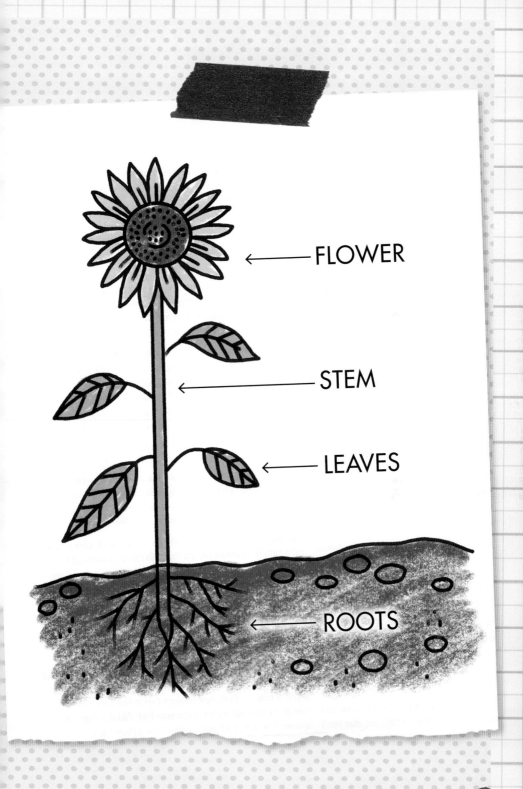

FLOWER

STEM

LEAVES

ROOTS

They use their **roots**! Just like us, plants need water and nutrients to grow. Plant roots grow into the soil where they soak up water and nutrients. But roots don't just help plants grow. They also help plants stand! Roots hold plants firmly in the ground.

Nutrients are found in the foods we eat. They are also found in the soil! They help both people and plants grow strong.

Fascinating!

Just like plants, roots come in many shapes and sizes. Some grow out in all directions and don't get very deep.

Other roots grow straight down and reach far into the soil.

Roots can give *us* nutrients, too!
Both potatoes and carrots are
roots that we eat.

WHAT IF PEOPLE HAD ROOTS?

The plant drinks with its roots. What happens next?

How do water and nutrients get from the roots to the rest of the plant? They move up the **stem**! That is one of the stem's big jobs.

Stems are filled with tiny tubes. Those tubes work like pipes, sending water and nutrients where they are needed. Stems can also store nutrients, like a kitchen pantry!

That is not the only thing stems do. Stems also hold leaves up to the sun.

Some kinds of plants have stems made of wood. These are called woody plants. Trees are a kind of woody plant. Trees have stems covered with bark. They are called trunks. A tree trunk sends water and nutrients from the roots to the leaves. Tree trunks are also very strong and help trees grow tall.

Thinking about plants makes
me hungry. I eat plants.

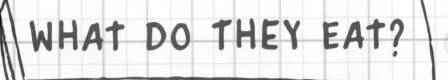

WHAT DO THEY EAT?

???

We get nutrients from food. Plants get water and nutrients from the soil. How do plants turn water and nutrients into food? They use their leaves! And the sun.

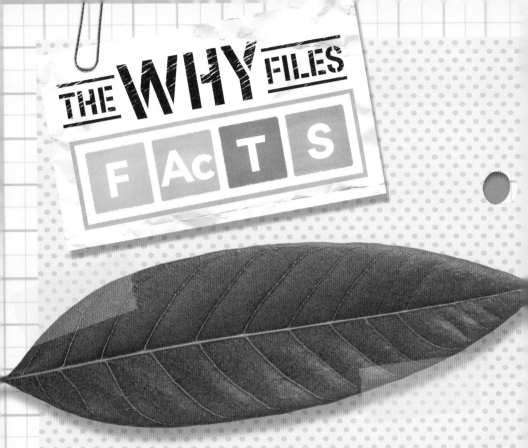

PARTS OF A LEAF

- The **BLADE** is the main part of the leaf where food is made.

- The **STALK** connects the leaf to the rest of the plant.

- Leaf **VEINS** are like small tubes. They carry water and nutrients from the plant stem to the rest of the leaf.

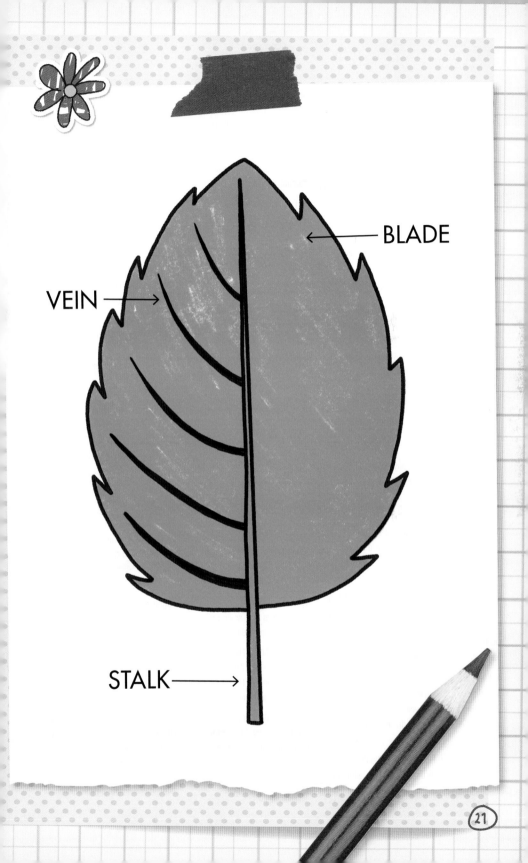

BLADE

VEIN →

STALK →

21

Plant leaves use sunlight, water, and **carbon dioxide** to make food. This process is called **photosynthesis**. Humans can't do it. Animals can't do it. Fungi, like mushrooms, can't either. Only plants!

PHOTOSYNTHESIS CHAMPION

I need water and food.

I need air, too.

DO PLANTS NEED AIR LIKE ME?

Plants need air to make food.
But plants use air differently than
we do.

We breathe in **oxygen** from the air with our nose or mouth. Then we breathe out **carbon dioxide**. In photosynthesis, this happens the other way! Plant leaves are covered with tiny holes called **stoma**. Just like our nose and mouth, stoma open to let air in and out of leaves. Plants take in carbon dioxide, and they let out oxygen. This is important for our planet. More oxygen means less air pollution!

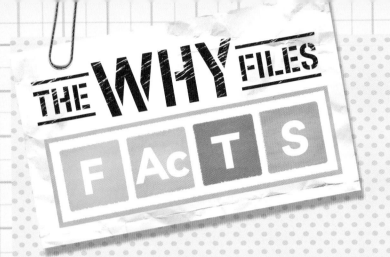

THE WHY FILES

FACTS

Many living things use plants for food. But plants have also been used by humans as medicine.

The Mohegan people used sap from **SUGAR MAPLE TREES** to treat sore throats. They also used it to make maple syrup.

The Incas made tea from a plant called MUÑA. This herb is full of vitamins, like calcium, that make bones and teeth strong. People in Peru still use Muña in tea and many other foods, like soup and stews.

The people of ancient Egypt used MINT to help clean their teeth and mouths. Mint is still used in toothpaste around the world!

Many plant leaves are green. Why?

Plants have a special pigment called **chlorophyll** (*KLOR-uh-fil*). Pigments are found in paint, too! They give color to the world around us. Chlorophyll turns light from the sun into plant food. It also makes plants green.

Not all plants are green. What about plants with red leaves? Or purple? Why are they different? Can they still make food? Yes! Their leaves also have chlorophyll. Photosynthesis is still hard at work. But these plants have other pigments, too. Those pigments can also turn light into food, but they make leaves look red or purple.

Awesome possum! I love the green trees in summer. Why do they turn colors in fall? Why do the leaves fall?

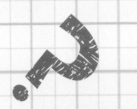

As the seasons change, there is less sunlight, and it gets colder. This makes the chlorophyll in leaves break down. Plant leaves that have only chlorophyll turn yellow. In leaves with many kinds of pigments, the other colors begin to shine! Leaves can turn red, orange, and purple in the fall. In time, those other pigments also break down. Then the leaves fall off the tree.

Goodnight until spring!

Leaves fall in the fall.

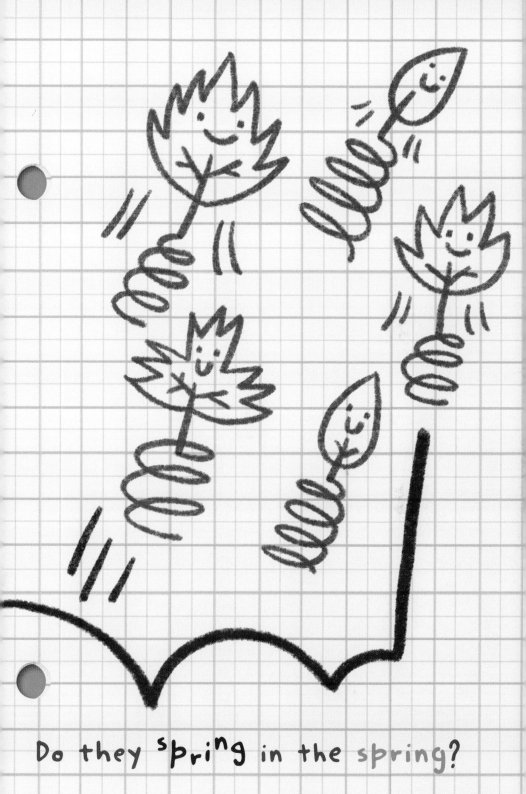

Do they spring in the spring?

Not all trees lose their leaves in the winter. Evergreen trees have needles for leaves. They only lose a few needles at a time. It happens during spring, summer, fall, AND winter!

PLANT

(a poem by Ada Twist)

Is it fun to be a plant?
There are things you can do.
And things that you can't.

You can soak up the sunshine.
Or climb up a wall.
You can be very tiny.
Or be very tall.

But you can't do experiments
or pedal a bike
or do anything else
    that I really like.
So instead of a tulip, a fig
    tree, or yam,
I'll keep
    being Ada.
Cause that's
    who I am!

My flower is beautiful.

BUT WHAT DOES IT DO?

Flowers have a very important job. They help to make more plants!

Most plants start out as seeds. That means plants need seeds to make more plants. Flowers have a special plant dust called **pollen**. When pollen moves from flower to flower, it is called **pollination**. And mixing pollen from different flowers makes seeds!

Pollen!

ALL KINDS OF SEEDS

SUNFLOWER SEED

PUMPKIN SEED

APPLE SEED

40

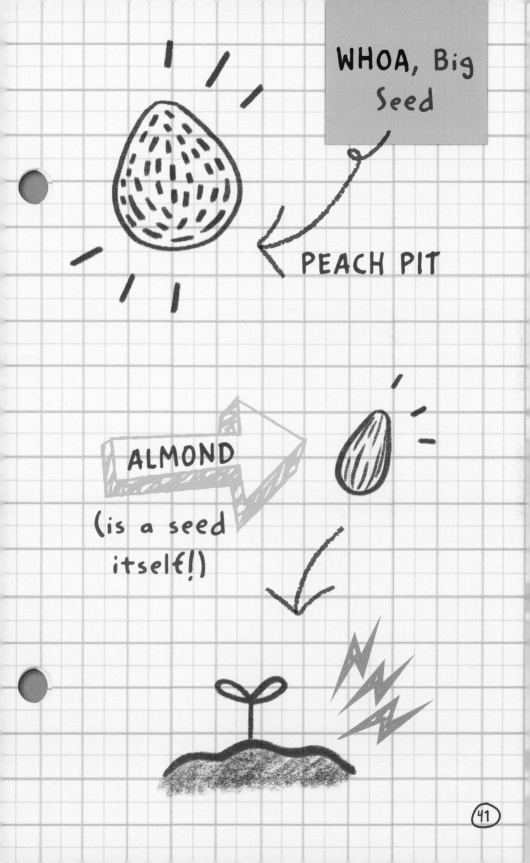

WHOA, Big Seed

PEACH PIT

ALMOND

(is a seed itself!)

41

But mixing pollen doesn't just make seeds . . . mixing it in the air also can make us sneeze!

43

Some flowers are small. Some
are big. Some are brightly
colored.

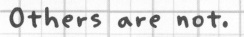

DO ALL PLANTS HAVE FLOWERS?

No! Plants like pine trees have cones. And just like flowers, cones release pollen! When the pollen moves from cone to cone, seeds are made.

Other plants don't have flowers *or* cones. Ferns use **spores** (sounds like *store* but with a *p*). Spores are also like dust. They form on the bottom of some plant leaves.

When spores from different plants mix in the soil, more plants are made!

- Some of the tallest plants in the world are trees that have cones. They are called **CONIFERS**.

- The smallest plant in the world is called **WATERMEAL**. Each plant is about the size of a single grain of rice.

- The oldest living plant is called **PANDO**. Pando is found in Utah and is around 80,000 years old!

- **PANDO** is also the largest living thing on Earth! From above, Pando looks like a huge forest.

But each tree comes from the same roots. Pando covers over 100 acres of land.

Wow! that is the size of about 53 soccer fields!!

How does pollen travel from flower to flower, or from cone to cone? The wind helps many plants spread pollen.

Other plants get a little help. They need bugs and birds!

There is a bee on my flower.

WHAT DOES IT WANT?

Flowers make **nectar**. Nectar is a mix of sugar and water. This sugar water tastes good to bees!

Bees fly from flower to flower getting nectar to make honey. As they buzz around, they also mix pollen between flowers. Hummingbirds also drink nectar and spread pollen from flower to flower. Without bees, hummingbirds, and other insects, many plants on our planet would not survive.

Naomi Fraga is a botanist—that
means she studies plants! Some
of the plants she studies live in
the desert. The desert is very dry,
so these plants get less water
than others and have ingenious
ways of staying hydrated.

WE NEED A BRAINSTORM

Bugs and birds are important for pollination. They help us grow food, and they need food, too! As we build more houses and roads, there are not as many flowers. But here's how we can help!

- Not all plants grow flowers at the same time. Having plants in your garden that grow flowers in different seasons can give pollinators food year-round!

- Pollinators use some plants for food and other plants for protection. Grow a patch of tall grass in your yard for them to hide in. Even grass in a flowerpot will work!

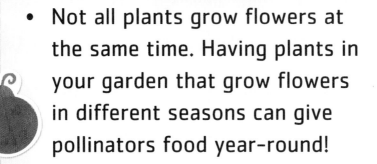

- Just like plants, pollinators need water. Putting out a birdbath will help them!

My flower smells so sweet. One time, I smelled a flower that was stinky like an old sock. P.U.!

Some flowers are stinky. Very stinky.

The ↑ Rafflesia flower

In fact, the largest flower in the world smells like rotten meat. Who wants to smell that? A fly! Flies like to eat almost anything. Even things that smell bad! Stinky flowers use flies and beetles to mix pollen.

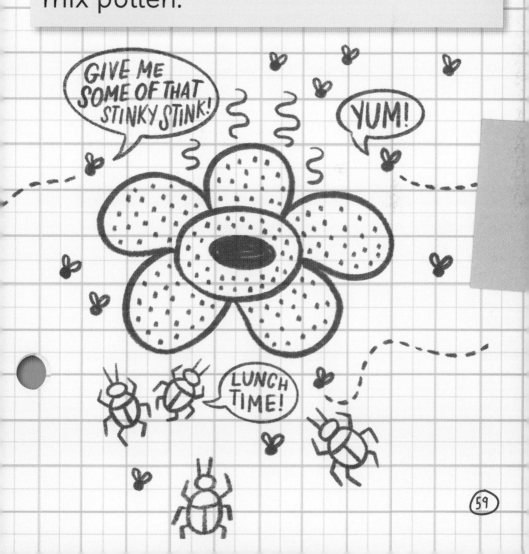

I found a seed in the crack of the sidewalk, too. Will it grow into a flower?

How does a seed turn into a plant? First, it needs to get to the ground.

Seeds can fall from flowers. People can also plant seeds in the ground. Seeds can even be pooped out!

Some flowers make fruit, and all fruit have seeds. When animals eat fruit, the seeds can pass all the way through their bellies and out the other end in their poop! The seed lands on the ground, ready to turn into a plant.

63

I have an idea! I'll put the seed into a pot of soil. Will it grow?

When a seed is in the soil, it needs water and oxygen to start growing. Air is everywhere. Even in the dirt!

Some seeds like the dirt to be cold, but some seeds like it warm or even hot! It has to be just right.

The first thing a seed grows are its roots. The roots take up water and nutrients. This gives the seed energy to grow a small plant. Once the plant gets bigger, it will grow out of the ground. These baby plants are called **seedlings**. They can now use photosynthesis to make their own food and grow . . . and grow . . . and grow!

JANE COLDEN was the first woman plant scientist in the United States. From 1753 to 1758, she collected information about hundreds of different types of plants in New York.

GEORGE WASHINGTON CARVER was one of the first Black American plant scientists. His work helped farmers learn the best ways to grow different kinds of farm plants.

THOMAS WYATT TURNER was the first Black person in America to earn a PhD in botany (plant science) in 1921. He studied how nutrients in soil change how plant roots grow.

MARIE CLARK TAYLOR became the first Black American woman to earn a PhD in botany in 1941. She researched how light changes the way plants grow.

I have MORE QUESTIONS now than I did before.

Why does each question lead to three questions more?

Is answering that what science is for?

MY QUESTIONS!

Do bees like yellow or red flowers better?

How did Native Americans figure out which plants were helpful?

Does moonlight help plants grow?

How do bees buzz?

How can I help the pollinators?

Do plants grow on other planets?

What is the deepest plant root?

How far can birds or animals spread seeds?

SIMPLE SCIENCE EXPERIMENTS

You can ask a grown-up for help!

ROOTS IN ACTION!

MATERIALS

- 3 clear cups (plastic or glass)

- Water

- Food coloring

- 3 celery stems with top leaves attached

- Ruler

- Knife

- Cutting board (optional)

INSTRUCTIONS

1 Fill each cup halfway with water.

2 Add food coloring to the water. About 5-10 drops should do the trick!

3 Stir gently.

4 Ask an adult to help cut ends off each celery stem. You will need to cut the celery short enough so that it doesn't tip over your cup when placed inside.

5 Put the celery stem in the cup with colored water.

6 Time to observe! You can take notes about how the stem looks at different time points after you have placed it in water. How does it look two hours later? What about four? Or twenty-four?

When you are finished, you can also cut the stem in half and observe the tiny tubes inside! What do they look like? Share your results on social media using #whyfileswonders!

LET'S TRY ANOTHER EXPERIMENT!

SPRING TO LIFE!

MATERIALS

- A small plastic zip bag

- One paper towel

- A few dry, uncooked bean seeds (like pinto beans)

- Tape

- A window

INSTRUCTIONS

1 The day before you begin, soak your beans in water overnight.

2 The next day, wet the paper towel with water and place it inside of the small zip bag.

3 Add the soaked seeds to the bag.

4 Close the bag and tape it to a window.

5 Observe! What do your seeds look like twenty-four hours later? What about three days later? A week?

You can run a few experiments at the same time! Tape one bag to a closet door and one to a window with sun. Which bag grows seeds the fastest? You can also compare different kinds of seeds. Which sprout most quickly? Share your results on social media using #whyfileswonders!

Andrea Beaty is

the bestselling author of the Questioneers series and many other books. She has a degree in biology and computer science. Andrea lives outside Chicago where she writes books for kids and plants flowers for birds, bees, and bugs. Learn more about her books at AndreaBeaty.com.

Sirk Productions

Theanne Griffith, PhD,

is a brain scientist by day and a storyteller by night. She is the lead investigator of a neuroscience laboratory at the University of California–Davis and author of the science adventure series *The Magnificent Makers*. She lives in Northern California with her family. Learn more about her STEM-themed books at TheanneGriffith.com.

Chris Lo Bue Photography

CHECK OUT THESE OTHER BOOKS STARRING

ADA TWIST, SCIENTIST

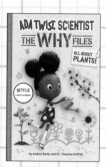

There's more to discover at **Questioneers.com.**